THE DAY THE UNIVERSE EXPLODED MY HEAD

POEMS TO TAKE YOU INTO SPACE AND BACK AGAIN

Allan Wolf illustrated by **Anna Raff**

CANDLEWICK PRESS

THE SUN
A Solar Sunnet, er, Sonnet

Born four and one half billion years ago,
I'm ninety-nine point eight percent the mass
of everything the solar system knows.
My gravity holds all within its grasp.

I watched as each young planet got its start.
I sheltered them inside my atmosphere.
I am the solar system's burning heart,
the light and life of everything that's here.

I lit the fires that made you what you are.
When times were dark, I rose above it all.
Next time you want to wish upon a star,
you need not even wait for night to fall.

The simple truth may come as a surprise:
the closest star is right before your eyes.

THE SUN DID NOT GO DOWN TODAY

No matter what the poets say,
the sun did not go down today!
The sun did not go down today!
It only just appeared that way.
I'll tell you what the real facts is:
the Earth is turning on an axis!

The Earth turns on its axis
like a dizzy, spinning, tilted top.
Each year, three hundred sixty five
complete rotations without stop.
And as it spins, we all stand firm
and ride it round with every turn.

The sun remains there in the sky
and waves at us as we go by
on our spherical, miracle merry-go-round.
So next time you notice the sun "going down,"
watch in awe, but don't forget:
The sun stays put. It's *you* who's set.

A MOON BUFFET

When you're a kid, they tell ya that
the moon is made of cheese,
like cheddar, gouda, Wensleydale, or Swiss,
ricotta, mozzarella, or
whatever cheese you please.
But *our* moon's not the only moon there is!

Our solar system is the home
to moons of every kind,
one hundred eighty-four of them and counting.
To set the record straight,
I've tasted all of them and find
what follows is an accurate accounting:

Ophelia's made of tacos
and Europa's made of Spam.
Callisto's made of meatballs and spaghetti.
Themisto's made of yogurt
and Belinda's made of ham.
Calypso's made of garlic shrimp confetti.

Hyperion is onions
with an inner apple core
encrusted with an almond-cocoa dust.
Ganymede is gummy bears
and gooey melted s'mores
encased within an oatmeal-cookie crust.

Pandora is a mixture of
fried clams and mac 'n' cheese
and frozen custard cake, but just a sliver.
And Puck's a blend of bratwurst,
candy corn, and black-eyed peas.
Prometheus is mostly made of liver.

And so you see how all these moons
are more than meets the eye.
They're not just boring, tasteless satellites.
Instead of sitting down to eat,
just look into the sky
to satisfy your lunar appetite.

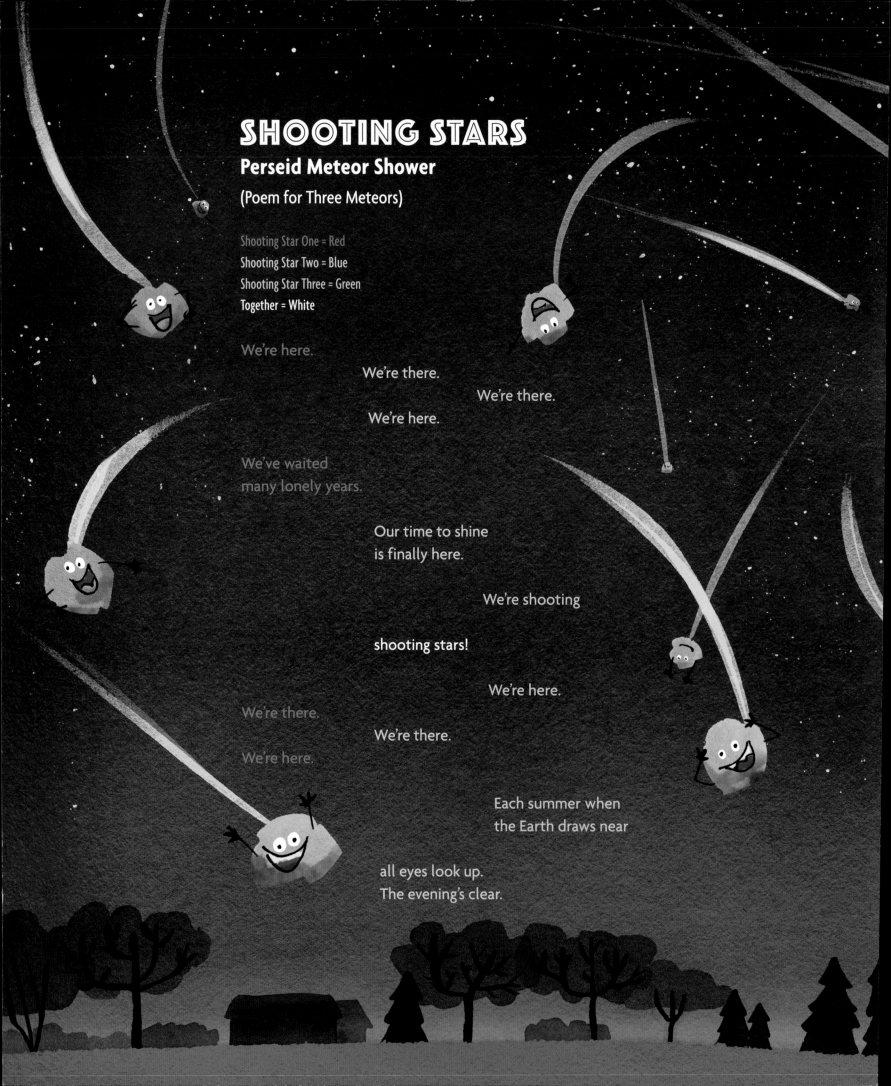

SHOOTING STARS
Perseid Meteor Shower
(Poem for Three Meteors)

Shooting Star One = Red
Shooting Star Two = Blue
Shooting Star Three = Green
Together = White

We're here.

We're there.

We're there.
We're here.

We've waited
many lonely years.

Our time to shine
is finally here.

We're shooting

shooting stars!

We're here.

We're there.

We're there.

We're here.

Each summer when
the Earth draws near

all eyes look up.
The evening's clear.

We skip across the atmosphere.

We're shooting

shooting

shooting stars!

We're children of the comet's tail
left lingering in Mother's trail.

Lone lumps of rock.

Spare specks of dust.

Miraculous.

Mysterious.

Now wish a secret wish on us.

We're shooting

shooting

shooting

shooting stars!

METEORITE

Chaos in Chelyabinsk
February 15, 2013

There was a blinding flash of light.
There was a sudden loud *ka-BOOM!*
The dogs all barked. The birds took flight.
The mayor calmly said, "We're doomed!"

The local townsfolk fled in fright.
The mayor calmly said, "I think,
if my close calculation's right,
all humans will become extinct!"

Chaos swept the city streets.
Dogs and cats became good friends.
Boys put down the toilet seats.
The mayor sighed, "This is the end."

Although there were some injuries,
there were no deaths. And luckily,
the townsfolk earned a fortune selling
souvenirs they made . . .
from pieces of the meteorite
that fell to Earth that fateful night.

MERCURY
Given to Extremes

Everybody look at me!
It's me! The planet Mercury.
As planets go, I'm number one
because I'm closest to the sun.
I may be small, but I stand tall;
my axis barely tilts at all.
Some find my temperament severe
because I have no atmosphere.
My days are four times boiling hot.
My nights will freeze your eyelids shut!
I orbit fast. I rotate slow.
I'm given to extremes, I know.
Unruly planet like no other —
the planets' pesky little brother.

VENUS
Come Live with Me and Be My Lunch

A polished pearl of light above,
I'm named for the Roman goddess of love.
The brightest planet in the sky.
Come live with me, and don't be shy.

Come live with me. We'll make it work—
although I have my little quirks:
I rotate backward from the norm;
no moons or rings adorn my form;
your Earth air makes me discontent
(I'm oxygen intolerant).

Come live with me, my darling dear.
I'll hold you in my atmosphere.
Just feel how it embraces us,
so heavy it can crush a bus!

Come live with me and stay forever.
Behold my roaring windy weather,
my craggy rocks and barren plains,
my sweet sulfuric-acid rains.

My gown is a poisonous shimmering cloud.
I'll wrap you in my stifling shroud
that traps in the heat as it blocks out the light—
nine hundred degrees of nonstop night!

A polished pearl of light above.
Come live with me and be my love.
But if you do, then hold your breath.
I'm venomous Venus. I'll love you to death!

EARTH
Your Mother I'll Be

I'm Earth. I'm your mother and cradle in one,
a love like no other in sight of the sun.
I offer you shelter, the whole human race.
I'll be your safe haven in vast lonely space.

My large iron core plus my speedy rotation
keep all of you safe from the sun's radiation,
creating a mighty magnetic force field
that causes the wild solar whirlwinds to yield.
And due to my ozone's thick UV deflection,
my atmosphere offers you sunburn protection.
I'm seven parts water, three other parts land.
I'll give you a drink and a dry place to stand.
I'll give you bright day, and I'll give you dark night.
My average temperature's just about right.
My equator is hot. And my ice caps are cold.
And I'm just over 4.5 billion years old.
But that's barely a baby in universe years.
Near eight billion people in both hemispheres,

without hesitation, I shelter you all:
the whole human race on a small blue ball.
You'll all be my baby. Your mother I'll be.
I take care of you. Will you take care of me?

MARS
A Martian Sonnet

I'm named for the Roman god of war.
But I haven't got a clue what for.
Just half the size of planet Earth,
I'm light of mass and slight of girth.
My volcanoes and canyons aren't really that bad.
I'm red 'cause I'm rusty, and not 'cause I'm mad.
Below I'm the color of butter. Above
I'm that orange-red hue that you all know and love,
all due to my atmosphere, rampant with rust,
which gives me my signature rubicund blush.
So don't believe all of that god of war hype:
I'm ten parts bark and no parts bite.
From afar I seem harsh, but I bid you "Shalom!"
Someday in the future, you may call me home.

THE MOONS OF MARS

Fear and Terror!

(Poem for Two Small Moons)

Phobos = Red
Deimos = Blue
Together = White

We're Martian moons. They call me Phobos.
And I'm his little bother, Deimos.
We're named for the gods of fear and terror.
But we're afraid there's been some error.
'Cause I look like a lima bean.
And I look like a baked po-tater.

JUPITER
I'm Jupiter the Giant

I'm Jupiter the giant.
The solar system's mayor:
I'm gas and wind and clouds wedged into
thick lasagna layers.

I'm Jupiter the giant,
King Kong of planetkind.
My mass is two point five times more
than all the rest combined!

I'm Jupiter the giant,
the planets' bodyguard.
My gravity keeps space debris
from landing in the yard.

I'm Jupiter the giant,
magnetic number one!
My loud and clear magnetosphere
is larger than the sun!

I'm Jupiter the giant.
Behold my Great Red Spot,
a beauty mark the size of Earth,
that rages round the clock.

I'm Jupiter the giant.
I'm master of the moons.
To introduce them all by name
would take two afternoons.

They orbit round my monstrous bulk
like planets round a sun.
I'm Jupiter the giant.
And I'm Planet Number One.

SATURN
And the Winner for Best Wardrobe Is . . .

I am Saturnista Fashionista:
famous, vain, admired, adorned, adored.
I want to thank the galaxy
for this overdue award.

From Sears to Saks Fifth Avenue,
they carry all my lines.
(Ever try a Hula-Hoop?
That's one of my designs.)

My rings are often copied,
but they never get it right.
The secret's in the extra ice
I add to catch the light.

The many paparazzi moons
that orbit round me stare
and quote the witty things I say
and note the clothes I wear.

I'm not very dense.
I'm a wisp of a thing.
Most planets consider me lucky.
I never take baths
'cause I always leave rings.
And I float like a toy rubber ducky.

Now, if you will excuse me,
I've got autographs to write.
Don't hate me 'cause I'm beautiful.
I love you all!
Good night!

URANUS
The Planet Behind the Blue-Green Mask

My poker face is featureless. I'm private and elusive.
I'm mysteries and puzzles all throughout.
But since you've traveled all this way, I'll make this one exception
and take you on a tour from inside out.

My rocky core's afloat within an ocean of ammonia
inside a sphere of superheated clouds,
where carbon turns to diamonds in a pressure-cooker sky
enveloped by a freezing methane shroud.

I rotate horizontally, reclining on my side!
My days and nights are forty-two years long!
I've counted twenty-seven moons and thirteen wispy rings
all running north and south (some think that's wrong!).

My surface isn't solid. There's no place for ships to land.
Just glimpse beneath my blue-green mask to better understand.
And look beyond my poker face. The treasures you'll discover!
Don't ever judge a planet by its atmospheric cover.

NEPTUNE
The Lonesome, On-My-Own-Some Neptune Blues

I'm so alone. So all alone.
I'm more than two point seven billion miles from home.
I want a planet playmate
I can call my very own.
I've got those lonesome, on-my-own-some Neptune blues.

Come out and play. I want to play.
I want a friend to keep my loneliness at bay.
I'm waiting in the outfield
for the ball to come my way.
I've got those lonesome, on-my-own-some Neptune blues.

My days are dark. It's always night.
From here the sun is just a tiny speck of light.
And my winds make it impossible
to ever fly a kite.
I've got those lonesome, on-my-own-some Neptune blues.

I had a spot. A stormy spot.
Just like the Great Red Spot that Jupiter has got.
But my spots never, ever stay.
They all just fade away
and leave me lonesome, on-my-own-some Neptune blue.

I've got some rings. Some ragged rings.
Up in the air. They're barely there, likes bits of string.
They say within a hundred years
my rings will disappear.
and leave me lonesome, on-my-own-some Neptune blue.

I'm the caboose. The blue caboose.
I try to harmonize alone, but what's the use?
They say my blue is caused by methane gas
But here's the honest truth at last:
my blue is due to lonesome Neptune blues.

I've got those hydrogen-methane-and-helium,
one-hundred-sixty-five-years-to-orbit-the sun,
march-to-the-beat-of-my-own-drum
lonesome, on-my-own-some Neptune blues.

THE MOONS OF NEPTUNE
Roses Are Red, Neptune Is Blue

When you're alone, pick up the phone.
'Cause you have fourteen faithful moons to call your own.
And even though we're very small,
we love you, warts and all.
As we orbit safe inside your comfort zone,

Throughout the years, whatever weather,
you can count on us to make the bad days better.
Just look up into the skies.
You sing the lead. We'll harmonize.
We'll circle round you, and we'll sing the blues together.

$$\left[\frac{\partial}{\partial t} + v.\frac{\partial}{\partial x} + a.\frac{\partial}{\partial v}\right] f = \frac{\partial f}{\partial t}\right) \qquad We =$$

$$m \qquad \qquad W_x = G$$

$$\nabla . E = \qquad \nabla . B = 0$$

$$\nabla \wedge E = \qquad \nabla \wedge B = M_0 j + \frac{1}{c^2}\frac{\partial E}{\partial t}$$

$$F = q\left(E + v \wedge B\right)$$

PLANET X

I'm one part theoretical.
I'm one part hypothetical.
I'm one part mathematical.
They call me Planet X.

I'm one part supercilious.
Another part mysterious.
One part you-can't-be-serious.
They call me Planet X.

I'm one part speculation.
I'm another part sensation.
Exploration, fabrication,
computation, estimation
And a bit imagination.
And they call me Planet X.

And whether I exist or not
is anybody's guess.

PLUTO AND CHARON

Dancing with the Stars

(Poem for a Dwarf Planet and Its Moon)

Pluto = Red
Charon = Blue
Together = White

They call me Pluto.

                    They call me Charon.

They say we're cold.

                    They say we're barren.

From way out here
the sun shines dim.

But I've got her.

                    And I've got him.

I never let her from my sight.
She is my steadfast satellite.

                    I never let him from my sight.
                    He pulls me close and holds me tight.

Here's something else
you may not know:
we love to dance
and do-si-do.

Our moves are

                    gravitational.

Our dancing is

                    sensational.

We spin together face to face
a swaying outer-space embrace.

                    Like Ginger Rogers

and Fred Astaire —
a twirling

                    dancing

cosmic pair.

TWINKLE, TWINKLE, LITTLE MAN

Twinkle, twinkle, little star,
How I wonder what you are!
Up above the world so high,
Like a diamond in the sky.

—Jane Taylor

Dear observant earthbound man,
Let me tell you what I am.
Born inside a nebula,
I'm older than Count Dracula.
Dear observant earthbound man,
Let me tell you what I am.

Dear observant earthbound man,
Let me tell you what I am.
Behold my beauty, but beware
my plasma, solar wind, and flares.
I'm like a diamond in the sky,
so bright I'll blind you in the eye.

Dear observant earthbound man,
Let me tell you what I am.
A nuclear-reactor bomb
of hydrogen and helium.
A mighty ball of burning gas
a million times Earth's puny mass.

Dear observant earthbound man,
Let me tell you what I am.
I'm not small, just far away.
And if you visit me one day,
make a wish and close your eyes —
just before you vaporize.

GOING THE DISTANCE

(Rap for Two Voices)

DJ Energy = Blue
MC Square = Red
Together = White

They call us DJ Energy
                    and MC Square!
Physics is our business.
              We're a relative pair.

We're a hit
        when you gotta git
                    from here to there.

                Now we're gettin' in yer face
                to tell you outer space
                is a really
        really
                really
        really
                really big place!

When you're measuring in space,
normal units won't do.
So we'll school you on a few
of the units we use:

Astronomical Units
(or for short, AU).

An AU is the distance from
the Earth to the sun —

more than ninety million miles,
and we've just begun!

1 AU

Longer distances are measured
by the speed of light.

You go the speed of light,
you better hold on tight.

Seven
times around the world
in the blink of an eye!

That's one
hundred eighty-six thousand miles
every second.
Every second.
Every second.
Every second!

If you go the speed of light
three hundred sixty-five days,
at the end of the trip
you've gone a long, long way.

That's the distance
astronomers call one light-year.
When you measure
'cross the Milky Way
from there to here,

you'll see the galaxy's
a hundred thousand
light-years wide.

We take it all in stride.
We're your galactic guides.

They call us DJ Energy
and MC Square!
Physics is our business.
We're a relative pair.

We're a hit
when you gotta git
from here to there.

For now we'll cut to the chase.
And tell ya outer space
is a really
really
really
really
really big place.

SOLAR ECLIPSE

(Poem for Dr. Jekyll and Mr. Hyde)

Dr. Jekyll = Blue
Mr. Hyde = Red
Together = White

Dr. Jekyll and Mr. Hyde
both gazed up at the daytime sky
and witnessed a solar eclipse pass by.
Said Dr. Jekyll, "What we've just seen
is a new moon moving in between
the Earth and the sun, and its shadow cast.
So the Earth went dark as the shadow passed."

Said Mr. Hyde, "Here's what *I* think:
I stared down the sun, and I made her blink!"

LUNAR ECLIPSE

(Poem for Dr. Jekyll and Mr. Hyde)

Dr. Jekyll = Blue
Mr. Hyde = Red
Together = White

Dr. Jekyll and Mr. Hyde
both gazed up at the nighttime sky
and witnessed a lunar eclipse pass by.
Said Dr. Jekyll: "What we've just seen
is our own Earth moving in between
the sun and the moon, and its shadow cast.
So the moon went dark as the shadow passed."

Said Mr. Hyde, "Here's what *I* sees:
the night took a bite of the full moon's cheese!"

BLACK HOLE

I once was
a bright star more
massive than the sun. Then I
puffed up like a fiery stellar bubble.
I collapsed into myself. And for a while I was
nothing but energy and heat. In a billion years, my
transformation was complete. I woke up with a heedless
need to EAT! Everything I used to be became tremendous
density. Like squeezing twenty elephants into a china cup. And
nearly instantaneously, this density became, in me, an ever-
growing gravity, insatiable and greedy, with a never-ending
need to draw entire galaxies, through a huge and ruthless
black galactic straw, into my merciless, boundless,
insatiable maw. Dust, comets, planets, stars, and suns.
My cosmic feast has just begun.
And nothing can escape my hungry might.
I am the dark devourer
of the light.

A SPUTNIK MOMENT
First Artificial Satellite
October 4, 1957

(Poem for Two Scientists)

U.S. scientist = Black
Russian scientist = Red

We will show we're the best
when we beat all the rest
in the race to be first into space.

Don't you see, in the sky,
that strange light blinking by?
It appears you've come in second place.

IVAN IVANOVICH
Mannequin Cosmonaut
March 1961

Ivan Ivanovich,
mannequin cosmonaut,
loyal, consistent, and tirelessly trained.
Calmly reliable. Patiently pliable.
Tossed from a rocket and never complained.

THE CHILDREN OF ASTRONOMY

"The stars are much too far away,"
said Galileo Galilei.
"I've built myself a telescope
to see them closer up, I hope."

He bowed his head as if to pray,
and Galileo Galilei
looked deep into his telescope
and saw the moon and stars up close.

So Galileo Galilei
showed all the rest of us the way.
The Father of Astronomy
has lots and lots of company.

Like . . .

Tyson, Leavitt, Sagan, Oort,
Cassini, Brown, and Bessel.
Hawking, Halley, Hubble, Herschel,
Messier, and Mitchell.
Isaac Newton, Albert Einstein,
Kepler, Kuiper, Ptolemy.
Nicolaus Copernicus,
and, finally, there's you and me.

'Cause even average yous and mes
and hes and shes and us and wes
can watch the star-bright nights away
like Galileo Galilei.

FOR THOSE WHO LIGHT THE CANDLE

**For the astronauts and cosmonauts
who have given their lives to travel into space**

Since humans first looked up into the skies,
they dared to dream of someday going there,
to rise among the angels and survive,
and then return with wondrous tales to share.

With each success, a thousand futile tries.
A calculation wrong, a botched repair.
Yet in the face of failure, we still strive.
A burden that we gladly choose to bear.

And yet there is a cost to every prize.
For every worthwhile journey, there's a fare.
A few who lit the candle gave their lives
but left their spirits lingering in the air.

For all who dare escape this ball of clay,
these brave ascending angels light the way.

THE ROCKET LAUNCH

Announcer/Mom = Red
Astronaut/Kid = Blue
Together = Black

TEN
I am a go
for main engine start.
NINE
I've got courage in my heart!
EIGHT
I feel the rocket boosters start.
SEVEN
I've trained my brain
to make it smart.
SIX
With nerves of steel,
I play my part.
FIVE
I'm feeling so alive!
FOUR
I hear the engines roar!
THREE
I think I need to pee.
TWO
I'm kinda hungry, too!
ONE
Oh, no. What have I done!

The engines growl.
We're go for launch.
Then Mommy howls,
"It's time for lunch.
Get off that log and come on in!
Don't *make* me count from ten again!"

THE RUSTY ROCKETS RETIREMENT GARDEN

Kennedy Space Center, Merritt Island, Florida

(Poem for Four Aging Rockets)

Redstone Rocket = Red
Atlas Rocket = Blue
Saturn Rocket = Black
Jupiter Rocket = Green

Said Redstone Rocket, "In *my* day,
I launched Alan Shepard,
the first American in space!"

Said Atlas Rocket, "In *my* day,
I launched John Glenn,
the first American to orbit the Earth!"

Said Saturn Rocket, "In *my* day,
I launched Neil Armstrong,
the first person on the moon."

Said old Jupiter Rocket, "In *my* day,
I launched a monkey!"

Said Redstone Rocket, "In *my* day,
my engines generated
75,000 pounds of thrust!"

Said Atlas Rocket, "In *my* day,
I completed four crewed orbital missions!"

Said Saturn Rocket, "In *my* day,
I sent twenty-four humans
to the moon in just four years."

"In *my* day," said old Jupiter Rocket,
"I launched a monkey!"

Said Redstone Rocket, "In *my* day,
we led the way
for the bigger rockets to come."

Said Atlas Rocket, "In *my* day,
we were the workhorse of
the Mercury missions."

Said Saturn Rocket, "In *my* day,
we launched communications satellites
and the Skylab Station!"

Said old Jupiter Rocket, "In *my* day,
*I launched a monkey in *my* day!"
"I launched a monkey in *my* day!"
"I launched a monkey in *my* day!"
"I launched a monkey in *my* day!"

* To be recited as a round

THE DAY THE UNIVERSE EXPLODED MY HEAD

(Poem for One Human, One Heart, and One Brain)

Brain = Blue
Heart = Red
Human = Green
Together = White

I wanted to ace the astronomy test.
My brain was near bursting with numbers and facts.
My heart was exhausted. I needed a rest.
So I put down the books, and I tried to relax.

As I lay on the grass looking up at the night,
I was drawn to the bright waxing moon in the east
with Jupiter looming just off to her right.
My heart nearly swooned at the visual feast.

But my brain couldn't keep itself still for one second.
My brain couldn't chill out, unclench, or relax.
My brain thought of space as a science-class lesson.
My heart painted pictures. My brain gathered facts.

Motion, mass, and gravity.
orbit, axial tilt, rotation.
Shooting stars and icy comets,
stellar clusters, constellations.
Solar wind, magnetic fields,
photons, light waves, radiation.
Nebulas of dust and cosmic
galaxy confabulations.
Small misshapen asteroids.
Planets of immense dimensions.
Endless emptiness and voids.
Distance beyond comprehension.

I heard a *bang!* And then a *whoosh!*
My eyes flew open wide.
I felt a jolt of wonderment
from somewhere deep inside.
My toes began to quiver and
my eyes rolled in their sockets!
My gut felt the sensation
of a hundred launching rockets!

I was overcome with dizziness
and tightly closed my eyes.
My head filled up with AWESOME,
and it swelled up to twice its size!

And then, from every part of me,
I felt a song of inner peace
that filled the growing places
of the space between my ears.
A mesmerizing melody.
A grand galactic masterpiece.
A solar-system symphony.
The music of the spheres!

My brain and heart locked orbits
and commenced to harmonize.
My heartbeat and the hands of time
began to synchronize.
My mind began to understand
the mysteries of the skies.
My heart began to comprehend
the truth before my eyes.
By now my head had grown
about ten times its normal size!

The universe poured into me.
My brain was overloaded.
It smoked and glowed red-hot. And then

        it actually exploded.

You can learn many facts about space from a book.
But nothing's as real as a firsthand look.
The words of my heart were felt, not said,
The day the universe exploded my head.

NOTES ON THE POEMS

The Sun

The sun is a star, and as stars go, it's of average size. Some stars are massive supergiants. The majority of the four billion stars in our galaxy, the Milky Way, are dim red dwarf stars, much smaller than our sun. This poem is an example of a Shakespearean sonnet. It has fourteen lines: three four-line stanzas followed by a two-line stanza, called a couplet. Its rhyme pattern is ABAB CDCD EFEF GG, and it's written in iambic pentameter — each line has five iambs (pairs of syllables with a dub-DUB rhythm, like a heartbeat).

The Sun Did Not Go Down Today

When I first realized that the objects in the sky only *appear* to rise and set due to the Earth's rotation, my whole perception of the universe changed. Even when I'm still as a statue on the Earth, I'm in constant motion — everything in the universe is in constant motion: rotating, revolving around other objects, racing outward in every direction.

A Moon Buffet

At nearly one-fourth the size of Earth, our moon is the largest relative to its host planet of all the moons in our solar system. The myth that our moon is made of green cheese began thousands of years ago and is born of the fact that the full moon looks like a wheel of cheese.

Shooting Stars

The Perseid meteor shower gets its name from the constellation Perseus, where it can be seen. It's created by a cloud of debris trailing the comet Swift-Tuttle, which orbits the sun every 133 years. Every year, in July through August, the Earth's orbit takes us through this cloud of tiny particles; when the particles collide with our atmosphere, voilà, a beautiful meteor shower, observable in the night sky. Meteors entering the atmosphere this way are also known as shooting stars.

Meteorite

If a meteor survives its fiery journey through the atmosphere and hits Earth, we call it a meteorite. On February 15, 2013, a meteor entered the atmosphere near the town of Chelyabinsk, Russia. Because of its low trajectory, it entered the atmosphere undetected, going about 40,000 miles/64,000 kilometers per hour, and exploded 17 miles/27 kilometers above the ground with the force of an atomic bomb. It broke apart in the explosion, and the smaller pieces that reached the surface became meteorites. Although this poem is a comic look at the event, the reality was serious. The resulting shock wave shattered windows and damaged buildings, and hundreds of people were injured (mostly by falls and broken glass). Luckily no one was killed.

Mercury

With its speedy orbit around the sun (just eighty-eight days!), Mercury is aptly named after the fleet-footed messenger of the Roman gods. Even though Mercury orbits quickly around the sun, this little planet rotates very slowly around its own axis. This poem is written in rhyming couplets.

Venus

The subtitle of this poem is a humorous twist on the opening line of a love poem by Christopher Marlowe, "The Passionate Shepherd to His Love." Venus looks bright when seen from Earth, but its surface is cloaked in continual darkness. My description of "nonstop night" is a bit exaggerated; conditions are more likely to resemble nonstop twilight. This poem is written in rhyming couplets.

Earth

We tend to forget that our own planet is, well, one of the planets. Earth is floating in space just like the others. Like the previous two poems, this poem is in rhyming couplets.

Mars

This poem is not a true sonnet. It does have fourteen lines, but the rhyme pattern is different from the standard and the lines have four pairs of syllables rather than the traditional five. I guess they just do things differently on Mars.

The Moons of Mars

Not every moon is a sphere.

Jupiter

Some estimate that Jupiter's famous Great Red Spot, a windstorm the size of Earth, has been swirling around for more than three hundred years! Since 1830, the spot has been observed continuously. In that time we've seen it change in color, size, shape, and speed. It seems to be slowing down.

Saturn

When it comes to fashion, Saturn certainly knows how to accessorize. Without its rings, Saturn would be as featureless as its neighbor Uranus. Saturn is probably our most recognizable planet because of those rings. Like other so-called gas giants, Saturn is massive (second only to Jupiter) but not very dense.

Uranus

Uranus is not really featureless. It changes slightly with the seasons.

Neptune

This is a blues poem. By repeating the first two lines of each stanza, this poem can be sung in the style called twelve-bar blues.

The Moons of Neptune

Another blues poem.

Planet X

Some respected scientists suggest that there might be a planet (not a dwarf planet, but a planet planet) far beyond Neptune with an orbit of 10,000 to 20,000 years! Some call it Planet Nine; some call it Planet X. But as of right now it is just a prediction based on complicated mathematical models.

Pluto and Charon

Pluto and Charon are actually what is known as a binary system. Instead of Charon orbiting Pluto as our moon orbits Earth, Charon and Pluto actually orbit each other. And if that weren't cool enough, Charon and Pluto are also locked in a tidal orbit, so they face each other as they rotate, just like two dancers holding hands with arms outstretched as they lock eyes and twirl around the dance floor.

Twinkle, Twinkle, Little Man

This is a spoof on a poem that is incorrectly attributed to the mythical Mother Goose. Jane Taylor's original poem, published in 1806, was simply titled "The Star." Another myth says Mozart first set it to music. He did not.

Going the Distance

In these modern times, most distances within our solar system can be determined by bouncing electromagnetic microwaves off an object and waiting for the echo. As objects get farther away (beyond Neptune), to determine an object's distance from us, scientists use a complex variety of mathematics, instruments, and observation to measure sight angles, brightness, and variations in light.

Solar Eclipse, Lunar Eclipse

Dr. Jekyll is a character from a book by Robert Louis Stevenson. He transforms from the very nice Dr. Jekyll into the very mean Mr. Hyde. The good side of Dr. Jekyll is eclipsed by the evil side.

Black Hole

Just trying to imagine a black hole can be a head-exploding experience! Black holes are very, very dense areas of space-time with such strong gravitational pull that not even light can escape! Astronomers now believe that there is a supermassive black hole at the center of most galaxies. Even our own Milky Way galaxy has one. This poem is called a shape poem or concrete poem, in which the form of the text represents the poem's subject. I attempted to draw out the poem's lines, stretching the length, the meter, the rhythm, and the rhymes as if stretching rubber bands. As a result, much of this poem's rhyme is internal rather than placed at the end of every line.

A Sputnik Moment

The early race to see if the USSR or the United States would reach space first was tense. The Soviets successfully launched the satellite Sputnik and crash-landed the first probe on the moon (1959), soft-landed the first probe (1966), and set into orbit the first lunar satellite (1966). But President John F. Kennedy made it a matter of urgent national concern that the United States be the first nation to land humans on the moon. Finally, the Americans had the right stuff when Neil Armstrong set his made-in-the-USA boot on lunar soil in 1969.

Ivan Ivanovich

The Soviets twice launched a mannequin, nicknamed Ivan Ivanovich, into space. Ivan was accompanied, on both flights, by a canine cosmonaut and various other animals. Inside Ivan's empty body cavity was an audio recording of a choir and a recipe for cabbage soup. This poem is called a double dactyl, because many of its lines consist of two dactyls. A dactyl is a three-syllable word (or a metrical foot) with a spoken stress on the first syllable — as in *Emily*, *lollipop*, or *basketball*. A double dactyl is simply two dactyls in a row — as in *Emily Dickinson*, *licorice lollipop*, and *basketball uniforms*.

The Children of Astronomy

Astronomers in the order mentioned: Galileo Galilei; Neil deGrasse Tyson; Henrietta Swan Leavitt; Carl Sagan; Jan Oort; Giovanni Cassini; Michael Brown; Friedrich Bessel; Stephen Hawking; Edmond Halley; Edwin Hubble; William, Caroline, and John Herschel; Charles Messier; Maria Mitchell; Isaac Newton; Albert Einstein; Johannes Kepler; Gerard Kuiper; Claudius Ptolemy; Nicolaus Copernicus.

For Those Who Light the Candle

A poem such as this, a grateful tribute to the dead, is called an elegy. This poem is also a special sonnet with a twist. Unlike the traditional alternating rhyme pattern (ABAB CDCD EFEF), the first three stanzas share a repeating rhyme pattern (ABAB ABAB ABAB). This pattern "braids" the stanzas together just as the spirits of these brave men and women are braided through the history of spaceflight.

The Rocket Launch

The countdown is probably the most recognizable verbal starter cue of all time. The countdown draws out the drama. The countdown intensifies the anticipation. The countdown tells us where we are, in time, to the very second. The countdown has also been used by generations of irritated Earthbound parents to warn their ill-behaved children before sending them to the moon, or to outer space, or at least to their bedrooms.

The Rusty Rockets Retirement Garden

While this poem has a humorous tone, the use of animals in space was and is serious business. On January 31, 1961, a chimpanzee named Ham performed complex tasks during spaceflight. Three months later, a human, Alan Shepard, did the same thing. Mice, monkeys, frogs, dogs, rats, rabbits, fish, spiders, a wide variety of insects, and, yes, guinea pigs have all made this dangerous trip. While some survived the journey, many did not. They did help open the heavens for safe human space travel.

The Day the Universe Exploded My Head

If it hasn't happened to you yet, it will eventually. You learn all these facts about space and distance and time and history and gravity and light speed and worlds beyond distant worlds. Then suddenly the facts become so huge and so obvious and so crystal clear, like a ray of sun through the clouds, that you are overcome with "Awesome!" Luckily your head doesn't really explode. But the image is a great example of metaphor and hyperbole.

Read this poem carefully a few times. You may notice that its beginning is formally structured, with a very tight ABAB CDCD rhyme pattern. As a writer, this rhyme scheme is much more difficult than ABCB, because the poet must incorporate twice as many rhymes. Then a fight "breaks out" between the brain and the heart: crafting versus creating. The two voices are arguing yet also merging. As the poem continues, the rhythm and rhyme patterns become looser, more playful.

GLOSSARY OF SELECTED SPACE TERMS

asteroid: a rocky celestial body, orbiting the sun in the asteroid belt, between Mars and Jupiter. They come in various shapes and sizes, from small boulders to the largest asteroid, Ceres, considered a dwarf planet.

asteroid belt: a band of rocky bodies gathered between Mars and Jupiter. The asteroid belt separates the inner planets (closest to the sun) from the outer planets.

astronomy: the study of the universe and the celestial bodies within it

astrology: a belief that the positions of the planets and stars determines the future

Astronomical Unit: a unit of measure equal to the distance from the sun to Earth, or 93 million miles/150 million kilometers

atmosphere: the gaseous area surrounding a planet

axis: the center around which a celestial body rotates

Big Bang theory: a model of the universe positing that it began with an explosion from a single point billions of years ago

black hole: a region of space where gravity captures all matter, radiation, and light

comet: an icy celestial body that begins to melt as it nears the sun. The resulting vapor is stretched out by solar wind into the comet's trademark "tail."

constellation: an arrangement of stars given a name

dwarf planet: a celestial body orbiting the sun that has rounded itself into a sphere but has not cleared its orbital path of space debris. Some dwarf planets, such as Pluto, even have their own moons.

eclipse: a celestial event when the view of one celestial object is blocked by another object (as a solar eclipse) or another object's shadow (as a lunar eclipse)

ecliptic: the plane on which a planet orbits

galaxy: a group of stars, gases, planets, moons, and space debris held together by gravity. Astronomers believe there may be more than 170 billion galaxies in the observable universe.

gravity: a physical force that attracts one body to another

International Space Station: a laboratory satellite orbiting about 205 to 270 miles/330 to 435 kilometers above the Earth. It orbits Earth about once every ninety minutes.

Kuiper Belt: First observed in 1992, the Kuiper Belt is a group of more than a thousand icy objects orbiting the sun at a distance of between thirty and fifty astronomical units. Pluto is in the Kuiper Belt.

light speed: the speed at which light travels in a vacuum—approximately 186,000 miles/300,000 kilometers per second

light-year: the distance light travels in a vacuum in one year—about 6 trillion miles/9.5 trillion kilometers

Local Group: a group of a couple dozen galaxies, to which our own galaxy belongs

magnetosphere: the area surrounding a planet or other celestial body in which its magnetic field has a dominating effect

meteor: a meteoroid that burns up as it enters the Earth's atmosphere; commonly called a shooting star

meteorite: a meteoroid that survives its passage through the Earth's atmosphere and impacts the Earth's surface

meteoroid: a particle from an asteroid or comet orbiting the sun; smaller than an asteroid

Milky Way: the galaxy in which our solar system is located

nebula: a low-density cloud of gas and dust in which a star is born

orbit: the path one object (say, a moon) takes around another object (say, a planet). Also the movement of one object around another.

outer space: the universe beyond Earth's atmosphere. What we call outer space generally begins at an altitude of 62 miles/100 kilometers above sea level.

planet: a celestial body orbiting a star. To be considered an official planet, the body must be spherical and have cleared all debris from its orbital path.

planetarium: a building specially designed to create an accurate representation of the nighttime sky

revolve: to move in a curved path around a center, as when one celestial object revolves around another

rotate: to turn around an axis, as a planet does; to spin. Some planets rotate clockwise. Some rotate counterclockwise. And they all tilt variously in relation to the plane on which they're orbiting (their ecliptic).

satellite: an object, natural or human-made, revolving around a planet

shooting star: a meteor

solar system: our sun and all the planets and other objects that orbit it

solar wind: particles given off by the sun in every direction. This powerful wind reaches speeds up to about 1.8 million miles/3 million kilometers per hour!

star: a large self-luminous celestial object that produces light through nuclear reactions in its core. As stars go, our sun is of average size.

telescope: an instrument that makes distant objects appear closer

theory: a guess, or possibility, based on known evidence, but not actually proven or witnessed

tidal lock: when an object (like a planet or a moon) takes the same time to rotate on its axis as it does to revolve around another object

universe: all existing matter, energy, and space, including all galaxies and whatever lies between them. The observable universe stretches into space 13.8 billion light-years away from us in all directions.

wormhole: Assuming that space-time takes the shape of folded fabric, wormholes are theoretical passages from one layer of fabric to another. If wormholes exist, they could be shortcuts in time and space.

INTERNET RESOURCES

Ask an Astronomer: http://curious.astro.cornell.edu
A personal favorite; run by volunteers from the Astronomy Department at Cornell University

International Astronomical Union (IAU): www.iau.org
The world's leading association of professional astronomers. These are the folks who officially recognize and name any new discoveries.

Kids Astronomy: www.kidsastronomy.com
Another fun and informative website for young people, as well as a good resource for teachers; part of the KidsKnowIt Network

National Aeronautics and Space Administration (NASA): www.nasa.gov
The Mount Olympus of space information; one-stop shopping for all your space knowledge needs

Solar System Exploration: https://solarsystem.nasa.gov
A fun clickable site with quick info and facts

Space Place: https://spaceplace.nasa.gov
An excellent website for kids (and grown-ups) who are looking for simple explanations

ACKNOWLEDGMENTS

Thanks as always to the amazing, professional, and talented shining stars in that constellation of shining stars called Candlewick Press. To this book's North Star, editor Katie Cunningham. To Hannah Mahoney, whose stellar copyediting kept me from saying many stupid things. To Lisa Rudden for her out-of-this-world design. And thanks, of course, to Anna Raff, whose illustrations capture the humor and heart that I felt as I wrote these poems.

Readers, guinea pigs, research assistants, and vocal test pilots: Jen Murphy, Daisy Wolf, Simon Wolf, Jameson Wolf, Ethan Wolf, Maryam Ajjoul, Evelyn Mitchell, and the beatbox stylings of Mars Mignon.

Thanks to the Astronomy Club of Asheville and to Lookout Observatory at University of North Carolina, Asheville. And Professor Britt Lundgren, UNC-A.

To my binary star-mate, Ginger West. And all of our wayward satellites: Jameson, Ethan, and Simon. And to Dwight Strickland: rock star, artist, astrophysicist, and janitor. I can hear Dwight now, strumming "Ziggy Stardust" in some faraway space nebula.

And thanks to the constellation of talented artists who write, read, anthologize, and publish poetry for young people. To each member of this mighty crew, I wish a special star for you. Astronomers and poets are not so different. Both see the world as if seeing it for the first time. And both observe our world up close, so we can better know our place in it.

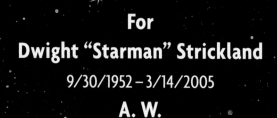

For
Dwight "Starman" Strickland
9/30/1952 – 3/14/2005
A. W.

For Dad
A. S. R.

Text copyright © 2019 by Allan Wolf
Illustrations copyright © 2019 by Anna Raff

First edition 2019

Library of Congress Catalog Card Number pending
ISBN 978-0-7636-8025-1

18 19 20 21 22 23 WKT 10 9 8 7 6 5 4 3 2 1

Printed in Shenzhen, Guangdong, China

This book was typeset in Agenda.
The illustrations are digitally assembled color collages,
made from sumi ink washes, salt, pen, and pencil.

Candlewick Press
99 Dover Street
Somerville, Massachusetts 02144

visit us at www.candlewick.com